THE BRIDGE

English translations of books by Marin Sorescu

POETRY

Selected Poems 1965-1973 (Bloodaxe Books, 1983),
translated by Michael Hamburger

Let's Talk About the Weather and other poems (Forest Books, 1985),
translated by Andrea Deletant & Brenda Walker

The Biggest Egg in the World (Bloodaxe Books, 1987),
edited by Edna Longley, translated by Ioana Russell-Gebbett
with David Constantine, D.J. Enright, Seamus Heaney,
Ted Hughes, Michael Longley, Paul Muldoon
& William Scammell, and by Michael Hamburger

Hands Behind My Back: Selected Poems (Oberlin, USA, 1991)
translated by Gabriela Dragnea, Stuart Friebert & Adriana Varga

Censored Poems (Bloodaxe Books, 2001)
translated by John Hartley Williams & Hilde Ottschofski

The Bridge (Bloodaxe Books, 2004)
translated by Adam J. Sorkin & Lidia Vianu

PLAYS

The Thirst of the Salt Mountain (Forest Books, 1985),
a trilogy of plays: *Jonah* (1968), *The Verger* (1970), *The Matrix* (1973),
translated by Andrea Deletant & Brenda Walker

Vlad Dracula the Impaler (Forest Books, 1987),
translated by Dennis Deletant

Marin Sorescu

THE BRIDGE

translated by
ADAM J SORKIN
& LIDIA VIANU

BLOODAXE BOOKS

ISBN: 1 85224 577 8

First published 2004 by
Bloodaxe Books Ltd,
Highgreen,
Tarset,
Northumberland NE48 1RP.

www.bloodaxebooks.com
For further information about Bloodaxe titles
please visit our website or write to
the above address for a catalogue.

Bloodaxe Books Ltd acknowledges
the financial assistance of
Arts Council England, North East.

Cover printing by J. Thomson Colour Printers Ltd, Glasgow.

Printed in Great Britain by
Cromwell Press Ltd, Trowbridge, Wiltshire.

To all who suffer.

MARIN SORESCU
1996

ACKNOWLEDGEMENTS

Acknowledgements are due to the editors and publishers of the following magazines and book, in which a number of these translations first appeared, sometimes in slightly different versions: *The American Poetry Review, Apostrof, Beacons, Branches Quarterly, Diner, Full Circle, The Mochila Review, Terminus, Three Candles, The Twelfth Street Review, and Gods and Mortals: Modern Poems on Classical Myths*, edited by Nina Kossman (New York: Oxford University Press, 2001).

This book is a translation of the complete text of Marin Sorescu's *Puntea: (Ultimele)*, published in Bucharest by Editura Creuzet in 1997.

Two poems, 'A Ladder to the Sky' and 'I Am Reminded of All Our Dogs', were translated by Adam J. Sorkin only.

Adam J. Sorkin acknowledges the generous support of the Penn State University College of Liberal Arts and the Delaware County Campus. As always, he adds thanks to Nancy, for careful reading, for good advice, for everything. Lidia Vianu expresses her appreciation to the Soros Foundation for an Open Society, Prague, for an award under the Research Support Scheme that supported work on these translations.

Poems with first-line titles in inverted commas were untitled in the original Romanian edition.

CONTENTS

TRANSLATOR'S FOREWORD

The eminent Romanian poet and playwright, Marin Sorescu, was his country's Nobel Prize nominee at the time of his premature death from liver cancer on 8 December 1996 at the age of 60. During the last two months of his life, he wrote prolifically. These poems, with their dedication, *To all who suffer*, are a testament not just to human mortality and pain but to resistance and triumph, a creative transformation of the struggle to accept fate and in the same breath defy its imminent finality. Sorescu composed poetry until the day before he died. Too weak to write, or, as the end came near, too downhearted – on his final day, he told his wife Virginia, 'I feel something that I never had before,' which she understood as a sign from him – he increasingly required her help to put on paper many of these valedictory works.

The Bridge is Sorescu's deathbed book, his consummation, and he of course knew this. Except for two poems inserted into the rest from when he was in a Paris hospital in October 1996, the volume progresses chronologically from the beginning of November onward. A mere five weeks. Most of the poems are dated, and the inexorable momentum of poem after poem toward Sorescu's death seems to make of the book something like a medieval tableau, a dance of death arranged as a procession of still living poems. The original version of *The Bridge* appeared in Bucharest in the spring of 1997 (its title in the Romanian language is *Puntea*, with a subtitle in parentheses, *Ultimele* – 'The Last', a plural form – which this translation drops). It was edited for publication by Virginia Sorescu, who for years served her husband as his assistant, typist, bibliographer, archivist, let alone (since she had worked at a printing press for decades) his book designer, typesetter and proof-reader.

In Virginia Sorescu's brief comment prefacing the collection, she notes that her husband Marin wrote many of the works 'on the pages of an old weekly appointment diary, 11 x 15 centimetres in size, with red plastic covers'. Then he would read them aloud to his wife, who typed drafts for him to work on. Here is Mrs Sorescu's description of the process of composition: 'The majority of the poems were dictated from this notebook to the author's wife, the author repeatedly revising and polishing the style while dictating. Other poems were dictated directly, without having first existed in a holographic version. There are poems, among the undated ones, that the author no longer had the strength to dictate.' At the climax of the sequence and dictated on the evening before he died – maybe reserved by the author and shared only on what he sensed was his last day (we can't ever know) – is the complex closing lyric, with its veiled allusion to Odysseus's Argos and, by extension, the idea of a homecoming, as fully realised a reconciliation as any poem in this volume reaches. On this same day, Sorescu rewrote the title-poem, 'The Bridge', introducing the line, 'I've never been so scared.' He was fully aware that, like Joseph Conrad, to whom he refers in an undated poem (Conrad also had deeply wanted the Nobel Prize but never received it), he himself had lost the race.

Throughout *The Bridge*, expressions of doubt, reluctant faith, protest, pain and despair mingle with what – as a translator and long-time reader of Sorescu's works – I see as gestures toward his characteristic ironic pose, flights into the fabulous and fanciful that, in context, are neither comically detached nor humorous in spirit. The blackness of the black humour is perhaps too urgent, too real. Within the world of the book, even given the parabolic, absurdist artifice of a substantial number of the poems, the poet's voice pro-jects a verbal space free of pretence. Sorescu's typically wry, dead-pan stance here turns inward and transparent. Many of the poems forego the playfulness of verbal irony (though the writer's situation is saturated with dramatic irony, every word defying the future); roughly three dozen of the 75 poems are spare and direct, as if in his final weeks simplicity became as expressive a tonality as the calculated ambiguity of poetic disguise and indirection.

It is the naturalness and transparency of Sorescu's style that in-evitably cause a translator most of his difficulties. But I found this was less of a problem in working on *The Bridge* than the inward division the process gave rise to in me. As translator, I experienced a strange emotional dislocation while revising the initial English versions Lidia Vianu provided for our collaboration. Not that I wasn't powerfully moved by Sorescu's imagination and his plight: I suspect that there is no way to be immune to the harrowing content, even if one tries. But translation is a special kind of read-ing, often demanding technical concentration curiously insulated from the images, the emotional charge, the meanings of the text. I kept finding myself solving a verbal knot, discovering what I felt was the precise, evocative word, sounding what my ear heard as just the right tone, and then breaking out with a smile of satisfaction grotesquely at odds with the depressing material. This was all the more disturbing because I admire Sorescu's poetry and drama very much and I was personally and professionally acquainted with him. I had met Sorescu at literary meetings on several occasions as well as at least half a dozen times in Bucharest, when I learned to know him as a warm and gracious host upon visits to his house, with the loyal dog in the entry yard and the concrete stoop on which he falls in one of the poems of this volume.

Yet I believe in a way that my divided reaction fits the intended impact of the poems in *The Bridge*. The book repeatedly gives rise to an emotional and artistic tension between, on the one hand, the pathetic and the sombre and, on the other, though not really in antithesis, the comic, the whimsical and the tongue-in-cheek. Marin Sorescu the genial, worldlywise man of the theatre, who in his poetry is always close by the lyrical persona, waiting in the wings for his cue, performs a beguiling, anti-heroic, anti-sentimental role before bringing the curtain down – and completely steals the show. His canny, seemingly guileless voice is paradoxically the mask of a hard-earned authenticity. Translating *The Bridge* ultimately became a humbling experience, an act of especial homage and respect.

During a visit to Virginia Sorescu with my co-translator Lidia Vianu, I have seen and turned the pages of the diary in which the manuscript was written, a 1965 weekly planner. Its disorderly entries were interfoliated with small scraps containing Mrs Sorescu's own handwritten jottings dating the poems insofar as was possible, along with some typed, reworked drafts. As I held this book, I found it impossible to ignore the coincidence that it had been kept for three decades from the year of Marin Sorescu's first mature collection of poetry, his straightforwardly entitled *Poems* that gathered some of his most celebrated and wittiest works and launched his career.

Then Sorescu was establishing his voice and technical mastery. It is almost as if these gifts are what sustained him as he arrived at the end. Even on the day before his death, when he could barely dictate, the artist inside the depleted human being took over (four poems in the book are dated 7 December). His wife Virginia told us that her husband stipulated changes even while she was writing his final poems into this appointment diary. She emphasised that, although in the editing process she had to place some poems where she herself thought they belonged and, presumably at the author's behest, omit some very bleak texts which, she added, would appear in later, posthumous collections, the organisation of *The Bridge* is as Marin Sorescu himself planned it. We have, of course, followed the order of the Romanian edition, including the page of addenda, five unused snippets from drafts of poems (the last, a succinct untitled poem in its own right); this book indicates the dates where they were provided in the original.

In a poem near the middle of the book, an apparently confessional Sorescu suggests that he is 'sorry / To have written you, my lines', and regrets that the lines of *The Bridge* 'might masquerade as poetry, / Were they not so desperately true'. In my heart, however, I cannot accept Sorescu's wanting his book to go unread. Quite the contrary. Throughout his life, he was foremost a writer, and such dissembling is part of dramatising the true and enduring. Moreover, the book is too well planned, advancing, for instance, from daytime in the opening poem to night in the penultimate, both with the poet in his sickbed, and then to the closing reference to a sort of passage beyond, though situated in a reminiscence. Virginia Sorescu mentioned that, near the very end of the process of composing this book and of his life, he reviewed and revised the first half of the manuscript. Thus I would like to think that this English translation of *The Bridge* is a way of calling out to the author with a kind of ovation, as Sorescu himself fantasises in one of the poems in the volume – translation in fact can do this, too – and 'for a moment' prompting him to claim his song and take a bow before he 'vanishes' again. My co-translator and I hope that this work in English is a worthwhile addition (let me borrow a phrase from a different poem) to the 'living library' of Sorescu's writings.

Lidia Vianu and I also hope the results of our collaboration would have been pleasing to Marin Sorescu, and we dedicate this translation to his memory, and likewise to Virginia Sorescu, who died an untimely death in the summer of 2001.

ADAM J. SORKIN

THE BRIDGE

Someone

Come to the sick man's bedside, sun.
Caress him on the cheek
With your warm ray, life's root.

Sky, haunted by so much cosmic energy
From thousands of suns and thousands of stars,
Such miraculous energy,
I implore you to lend me a sliver.
I have begged on bended knee.
If you won't give it to me,
Well, then, keep it yourself –
And stick it hard in your own eyes.

Gather round me, dear friends,
You too, God, come weep with pity.
Your sobs will do me good –
They're the sound of life.

Someone severs my ways
With a pair of shears,
Jeeringly patches them
And throws them to the dogs.

[1 November 1996]

Loneliness

Beside the sick man's bed,
Just the bedside –
He raises his head
And, as if he's noticed only now,
He asks,
'Have you come to sit with me,
Bedside?'

'Yes.
Someone must stay with you
During these long hours
Because you're so very ill.'

[2 November 1996]

The Bridge

I balance on something very frail,
A sort of precarious bridge
Blasted apart by the spasms
Of a fierce whirlwind.
A bridge between nothing and nothing,
Which I have not asked to cross.

I've never made
Such grotesque gestures,
Mimicking prayer, defiance, despair…
I'm hurled high in the sky
Among the thunderclaps,
I plummet here below,
Again I'm hurled above.
I've never been so scared.

'Get down from that
Imaginary line.
Don't you understand? It's all over.'
I'm tossed up yet again, slammed back to the ground,
My head whacked against the walls;
I totter, catch hold,
Barely stand on my own.
'I didn't know life
Was an imaginary line,' I say.
This buffeting makes sport with me
On the flimsy plank between earth and sky.

How far behind I've left the cradle,
Built of the same wood as the bridge,
In which my mother, singing and weeping,
Taught me the cosmic rhythm
I'm in the throes of losing now:
Hush-a-bye! Sleep tight!
'Why didn't you ever tell me that life
Was an imaginary line,
Mother?'

[2 November 1996]

Stop

'Stop!'
The soul screamed,
'Stop! I need to get off!
I've had my fill of duties,
So many responsibilities, obligations, laws.
I was meant to be free.'

'I cannot stop,'
The earth answered
(The earth in me).
'Get off however you can –
If you're up to it –
And hop to it lickety-split
While I revert
To disgust and clay.
Get off in the sky,
My lifelong friend.
I'll carry you back when I return.'

[2 November 1996]

Lord!

Lord,
Take me by the hand
And let's go! Together we'll run away
From this world!
Let's duck out for some air.
Maybe with a change of scene,
I'll feel more in my element
By Your side.

Cochin Hospital, Paris
[10-11 October 1996]

Inhabited Liver

I feel the wings of the eagle
Stretch wide the lips of my liver;
I feel the talons,
The iron beak,
The enormity of its hunger for life,
Its thirst for flight
With me in its talons.
And I fly.

Whoever said I was chained?

[2 November 1996]

The Masks

In unbelievable torment
I've experimented with
Seven, eight masks of death.
All of them I found terrifying.

I couldn't recognise myself.
'Take them away! Immediately! They upset me.
No, no, they aren't me
(Not even dead).'

I, who wept mighty sobs
Over the ruins of civilisations,
Over the rubble of clay tablets
And glazed bricks,
Why shouldn't I weep today, as well,
Over the ruins of my own stubbled cheeks?

[5 November 1996]

Reisefieber

My whole life long, I've suffered from *Reisefieber*.
So how will I make do in the skies
Rambling among the stars
With my ill-omened *Reisefieber*?

Even if I become a speck of dust,
I'd still drive the universe mad
(Oh, poor man, constantly on the move)
With my star-crossed
Restlessness for departure...

[5 November 1996]

The Departed

He left without making sure
He'd shut off the gas
Or tightened the water tap.

He didn't turn around at the gate
Because his new shoes were pinching him
To put on his old pair instead,
Or because he'd forgotten something.
Now he can't have forgotten anything.

He stepped past his dog
Without saying a word.
The animal wondered, then felt at ease:
'It means he's not going far.
He'll be coming right back.'

[5 November 1996]

A Ladder to the Sky

A spider's thread
Hangs from the ceiling,
Directly over my bed.

Every day I keep track of
How much closer it descends.
'Look,' I say to myself,
'I'm being sent a ladder to the sky,
Lowered from above.'

I've grown dreadfully thin,
A mere ghost of what I used to be,
Yet I think my body
Is too heavy still
For this delicate ladder.

'Soul, you go ahead.
Shhh! Shhh!'

[5 November 1996]

Ascites

And all at once
My ankles are missing.
My lithe, sprightly ankles
Have become entombed in folds of flesh.

My calves are like two ingots.
I stand on rough-cast pigs of rust and
Scrap iron.

My belly alone
Projects ahead of me,
As if ready for imminent birth.

Purling mysteriously within,
Water entices death:
Oh, come bathe!

[6 November 1996]

Spectator

I watch with great interest
How the instinct of life battles
Against the genius of death.

Life comes up with a thousand stratagems,
Death has a thousand and one feints –
Like two gladiators,
One with trident and net,
The other with a short sword.

Squeezed between the mysterious logic
Of life
And the mysterious logic of death,
I am their battlefield.
Only my eyes
Are left of me, to see
And glaze over with horror.

[6 November 1996]

'I'm on life's side!'

'I'm on life's side!'
I shout from time to time.
'Bravo! Bravo!'
Life raises an eyebrow at me, parrying
A trident blow.
'I'm rooting for you, life!'
'Hooray, I'm for this life – I don't know of any others,
Whatever and however they may be.'
'Monster, haven't you heard me?'

'He still cares for me,'
Life sighs.
Then to me:
'In fact, the one who does battle here,
So stalwart,
Is you yourself.
Don't give in! Take up your sword!'

Pure Pain

I don't feel ill in order to feel better,
I feel ill in order to feel worse.
Like the sea with its green, treacherous waves,
You cannot sound the bottom of pain.

I dive into pure pain,
Essence of scream and despair,
And I return to the surface blue and pale,
Like a diver who lost
His oxygen tank.

To the emperor of fishes, I beg,
Kindly send me your most trustworthy shark
To cut short my passing.

[6 November 1996]

28

Prometheus

Look, if you really want to cheer him up,
Ask him to give you a light.

His face, disfigured
In the battle with the eagle,
Will fall for a moment,
Then brighten,

As if he were smirking at Zeus:
You see, I'm still quite useful to people.

'And what should I do with the fire
That you gave me, Zeus,
The perfidious spark, painful,
Human?'

'Put the flame to your pyre,
The one you're bound upon.
Though extinguished,
It goes on consuming you, anyway.'

'Why am I the one who must enter this hospital?'

Why am I the one who must enter this hospital
While that man passing by at this very moment
Can proceed on his way?

Why should he so carelessly pass by the gate?
Why must I, of all people, enter it?
Why not he, why not someone else?
Why me?

Questions not yet answered.

Cochin Hospital, Paris
[10 October 1996]

Forerunners

I love my forerunners.
I feel toward them
A profound sentiment of piety and admiration,
No less for the fact that they died
Than for their having lived.
They were capable of dying.
They found the extraordinary resources
To fight against the eternal night
That in anguish they alone knew.
They faced it like a man
And breathed their last.

Now, as I prepare myself to become one of them, too,
In piety I kiss the shades of my forerunners.

[9 November 1996]

Vocal Extinction

The angel who sounds
Vocal extinction
Lifts the trumpet from his lips
And rebukes me
Because I'm expiring too quickly.
'Suddenly my voice seems to be vanishing.'
'Let it vanish only after you hear my trumpet.

'For you the trumpet hasn't yet sounded.
Go to the front ranks, soldier, and sing out.
Sing life.
You must still march on as part of it,
Raw recruit of pain.'

[9 November 1996]

'What hurts the worst'

What hurts the worst
Is that no longer will I be able to
Have contact with books,
To stand in front of my bookcase every morning
As on the shore of the sea
Caressed by secret breezes gently blowing
From the shelves.

Since I'm to be so close by,
O Lord, I hope I won't be denied
The pleasure of reading the stars

Once a week, at least,
According to the schedule posted on a cloud.

[9 November 1996]

The Emissary of the Blue Sea

'I hereby recall the water from your cells,'
The sea sends me word
Via an emissary.
'I have a need for fuel
(On the threshold of winter).'

'Now I understand why for some time
Dark clouds have hovered above me:
Within them there's a large part of myself
Waving goodbye.'

[9 November 1996]

'I look so dreadful'

I look so dreadful
That I waste a lot of time
Consoling those
Who visit me.

They wail, hide their eyes with their hands,
Then curse.
'Why you, of all people?' they blurt out.
'God, where can You be? Do You exist?'

I try to boost their morale.
'Well, never mind, it's not as bad as you suppose.
Last week I looked rather worse.
A sickness is a sickness, no getting around it.
It destroys whomever it inhabits.
And in the end, you know, we all die.
As Hamlet put it, "If it be now,
'Tis not to come."'

If it weren't for the dreadful pain,
I'd even accept this pose of the torture victim
With lamb-like serenity.
People mean well,
They're truly suffering for me.
'Be brave!'
I hear from all sides.
What else can I be?
I comfort everyone as best I can.
Only – I've no idea what more to tell myself
When I'm left alone.

[11 November 1996]

Wake

I'm a witness at
My own
Wake.

I don't know what to make of
The living me.
I don't know what to make of
The dead me.

I haven't yet handed him the message
Of this world.
He won't divulge to me the code
Of the world beyond.
(And, oh, we were like brothers).

[11 November 1996]

The Cowardly Coffin

It let itself be laid carefully in the grave
By skilled, brawny men
Inured to this.
('Hold it there! A bit more to the right!
That's it, OK! Let go! No, no, not all the way.')

When I finally touched bottom in the grave
(It had to be widened, since they dug it rather narrow),
The coffin gave a quick shudder,
A start,
And shot high above
Dragging the gravediggers along,
Caught in the straps.

The procession was astounded.
What material could the coffin be made of?
Or was there something horrifying
At the bottom of the grave?
The newspapermen required a clarification
And blamed the upcoming elections.

The coffin, which appeared quite ordinary,
Rough-planed planks nailed with 10-penny nails,
Knocked over several crosses,
Banged into the church steeple,
Swung about through the air
(The gravediggers climbed down from trees,
A plum or two in their mouths),
And after a while returned,
Contrite, to the rim of the grave.
It waited for flowers to be thrown,
And fresh earth.

The women, beginning to weep all over again,
Filed by it.
'Let's get with it, man! Give it another try!
Play out some more rope,
And you, you hold it down.

Two of you men sit on its lid
To make it heavier.
Others of you, jump on when it touches the ground,
As counterbalance.'

A little this way, a little that way, very carefully,
It descended like lead to the other world.
Then a sudden tremor –
And with a sort of stifled moan,
The narrow end first, as if from a launching pad,
Aerodynamic, it blasted off again.

As late as nightfall, with all manner of tricks,
It would not be buried.
Now it's flying crazily in the sky,
Soon to be shot down
By some rocket or another
From our missile defence.

[11 November 1996]

Balance Sheet

I have two serious diseases,
A few others, extremely serious,
Plus three more, no less than dreadful
(Every one, I've been assured, is incurable).

Each hurts in its own particular way.
An acute, differentiated pain,
Requiring all my energy
And power of resistance.

In sum they add up to a kind of
Essence of torture and anguish,
Something unimaginable.
I am played like a cursed organ,
Assailed around the clock
By a thousand tempests.

[11 November 1996]

Author

When I really like a book,
When I'm filled with enthusiasm,
I start clapping and calling out,
'Author! Author!'

I can't seem to suppress
This old habit
Of the man of the theatre.

The clapping intensifies,
It grows into a lengthy ovation,
And sometimes the author makes an appearance
At a corner of the bookcase.

A very modest man,
Quite different from how I imagined him.
Solemnly, he places his hand over his heart,
Bows shyly.
We look each other in the eye for a moment –
Then he vanishes.

In this way I've come to meet
Many of the writers
Who are the glory of libraries.
I met them in person.
They were in my house.

[19 November 1996]

The Book of the Dead

Absentmindedly he signs
The book of the dead.
The book of the living was removed,
Quite discreetly, not long ago,
And burnt with a gentle flame
In front of his house.

Whoever wanted to watch
Might watch, baring his head.

A little blood runs on the page –
The mourning angel dabs at it with a blotter.

[19 November 1996]

The Fall into Myself

My eyes have sunk
Into the darkest depths of my head.
'I'm going to bring my eyes back alive
From the darkest depths of my head,'
I announce one morning.

'It's a very long way.
Don't delay dinner for my sake.'

[19 November 1996]

Genetic Dowry

I'll surely have to correct
My many defects
There, in the beyond.

Foremost among them,
The longevity problem:
No longer may I contradict
Statistics,
With hope for life at birth.

Dwelling on a speck of dust
With a window to the sea,
That rests on another speck of dust
With a window to a mountain,
Springing up from the very core
Of yet another speck of dust,
I'll enjoy free access to divine landscapes.
My return ticket:
Hitchhiking on a sunray.

[19 November 1996]

Prometheus Unwell

Benefiting from the eagle's
Concentration as it stabs its beak deep within
And eats its fill,
He seizes its claws and scratches
His skin fast and hard.
'How lucky they're still so long!
My own nails have become blunt over the years,
Trying to soothe my nerves.'

Liver trouble gives you pruritus,
The fiercest itching.

[21 November 1996]

Prayer

God,
I'll climb onto a chair
So You may slap my face.
And look here, I've turned my other cheek.

Slap me hard, with all Your might,
Unbalance me forever,
Set me spinning to roam the universe
Like a new planet of pain,
A fiery ember hissing through the ether.

Let me not remain in torment.
Bring me the relief of Your terrible frown
And Your fierce anger
In Your great goodness.

The drop of divine essence
May be viewed from down below,
Emitting light, emanating happiness.

[21 November 1996]

Almost a Pantomime

She thrusts a dagger into her breast
As deep as the hilt,
Pulls it out, hands it to her betrothed,
Smiling.

'It doesn't hurt!'
He takes the dagger,
Stabs it into his breast as deep as the hilt,
Pulls it out, hands it back to her.
Indeed, it doesn't hurt.

She takes the dagger,
Tries to stab herself again.
But her hand clenches stiff.
The dagger drops, she dies.

'It doesn't hurt!'
He barely manages to say
As he reaches to retrieve the dagger,
Staggers, dies.
No, it didn't hurt.

I pick up the dagger,
Look at it
And start howling.
It hurts, it hurts awfully.
Brethren before me,
Why did you say it doesn't hurt?
It's one of those things that hurt awfully.

I turn my back and exit the stage.

[21 November 1996]

Concerning the Halo

The novice angels,
After they have sworn the oath,
Are briefed
About the halo
With which they've been newly equipped.
'It's not just the crown of glory around the head,
It's also the nimbus around the body.
It's a matter of a body around the body,
It's a matter of an aura.

'It can be lost, stolen, shattered,
It can be completely dispelled –
Which means disease and death.

'Exert your utmost care to keep it intact,
So as to stay lively, beautiful, happy,
With the will to do good forever and ever.

'Every day it gathers the dust and lint of evil energies.
In the evening the toilet of the halo must be performed
(There are various techniques).

'In general you dissociate
Into deep meditation,
Allowing the divine white flame
To channel through you.
Then sweep up the residue
And take it out for burial
In the earth's core.'

'Do people, too, have halos?'
'Of course they do,
That's a very pertinent question.
But their halos are puny,
Uncelestial, highly perishable.
Cast your eyes upon this man
Slowly approaching, hunched over

And sad. Of his halo
Only a few sparks were left,
And they could no longer protect him.'

[21 November 1996]

The Birds

I was making my way in the sky,
On foot.
I'd missed the celestial vehicle.
It had departed right under my nose.

The landscape was the same as you know it:
Stars shining bright,
Stars burning out and falling,
Meteors, comets.
It seems nothing ever changes
Here at the outskirts of our galaxy.
And when I looked back,
I saw birds, a myriad of birds,
I couldn't begin to count them,
Flights, flocks, always behind me,
Hilarious and obstreperous.
Like seagulls in the wake of a ship
That stirs up shoals of fish,
They were flying and eating something,
A sort of grain
That kept flowing out of my pockets.

An immense train of birds like a slipstream,
They propelled me forward with powerful wings.
Aha, I said to myself, that's how I'm able
To make my way in the sky,
On foot.

Then one of them approached me
And confided:
'Actually, we're not birds at all,
We who follow you everywhere –
We're your song.'

[25 November 1996]

49

At the Front

When my brother came back from the front,
He told me about an incident
I keep reflecting on
These days, I don't know why.

It was the middle of an offensive:
The wounded in the first ranks
Appeared among the trees
In their pools of blood and woe
Like a sort of lichen stain
Pointing the way to the front.

Some, badly smashed,
Could no longer move.
They screamed and cried out for water,
Repeated their addresses as loudly as they could,
And beseeched that their sad state of affairs
Be communicated home.
Others, their guns not far off,
Wanted to kill themselves
But could no longer
Reach the weapon.

You heard them everywhere around you,
Begging the gray soldiers,
Who frowned above their bayonets
And advanced with determined strides
And faith in God:
'Shoot me, my friend, shoot me!'
The dying men pleaded in dying tones.
And my brother added:
'Once I even stopped beside a man
Who lay beneath a tree,
His belly torn open by a shell.
"Shoot me, my friend!
Let it be over more quickly."'

'Seeing how things were,
I carefully readied my gun.
But then I glanced a single time at his face –
A child's – our eyes locked for an instant,
And I hastened to flee.
"Please!"
"Friend, it's not in me to be your executioner.
Wait, soon the stretcher bearers will show up,
They'll take you to hospital, you may be saved,
God can do anything."'

I wonder how hard a heart
God must have,
If He can stand to see the harrowing pain
Of the wounded forgotten beneath the trees.

[25 November 1996]

Ancestors

I've been aging unspeakably fast
In recent months, as others over several years.
Within one short year, from a man in his prime,
I've turned into an old man, an ancestor.

I understand now why your feet trip on the carpet,
Why you must walk humped over,
Why objects all come at you
And pester you,
Why you're reluctant to get out of bed,
Why more and more often you experience
A faltering and a forgetfulness
(As my poor mother used to say,
May she rest in peace:
'Lordy, I don't know what I've got,
I feel a vague faltering, an odd forgetfulness').
And why food loses its taste
As if you were chewing straw.

Why your wishes grow dim,
Your ambitions burn out,
Your senses always seem dozing...
I believe there's a *standard* that must be met there,
For everyone who arrives to have
An identical physiognomy
And be equally old.
Even a child, if he lies ill for a year,
Departs humped over and wearing the mask
Of a 70-year-old.

I've exchanged my pen for a staff.
I stumble. All the things in the house
Have turned threatening
And waylay me.

[27 November 1996]

The Three Kingdoms

Clutching a quartz crystal in one hand,
A blade of knotgrass and a leaf
Of plantain in the other,
I try to support myself as if on a pair of crutches
Along a rutted, rugged road.
I found my hopes on these two distinct kingdoms,
Which have always been well disposed toward me.

Oh, how pure a crystal I should have been,
Uniformly concentrated and transcendental
On every facet!
Oh, how useful I should have been to those around me,
Like the modest plantain,
Or the luxuriant tufts of knotgrass in the ditch.
The pigs detect me defiling their domain.
Extraterrestrials have a fix on me,
For they too are crystals.
But I limp on,
A man of flesh and blood,
Supporting myself on medicinal herbs,
Long-ago alchemised matter –
I limp down this road
Without horizon,
Mere man of flesh and blood,
My consciousness inflamed by knowledge,
Inappropriately animal.

[27 November 1996]

First Fall

I had no idea that in a fall
I'd gather such speed
And become so massive.
I'm a bolide, a meteorite.
In my helplessness I stumbled
And fell climbing the stoop at home.
For a long time I'd feared exactly this.
I'd expected it, dreadfully worried:
'You could hurt yourself,
Crack your skull –
Take care on the steps.'

Whenever I headed out the door,
I was urged to wear
A metal helmet
As though I were going to the front
To dodge bullets,
Or to work on a building site
Under scaffolding.

The helmet is inordinately heavy.
The force of gravity beats down on it
Like torrents of rain
And pushes me into the ground.
Whenever I can, I replace it
With a cardboard circle.

[27 November 1996]

The One Who Never Shows His Face

He had sojourned so long
In close proximity to the miracle
That he came to recognise God
From behind.

'Look at Him – there!' he suddenly exclaimed;
'It's He. I know Him.'
'Well, but that's a mountain.'
'That's how He appears, from behind.
Broad-shouldered – I know Him very well.'

And again: 'That stream flowing our way
Is He, from behind. What strength, what majesty!'
'But if it's flowing our way, that's from in front…'
'No, He walks backwards…'
'But have you ever seen His face?'
'No one's ever seen His face,
But I've begun to recognise Him from behind…

'He is everywhere. Turned backwards,
He advances in all directions.
There He is, at last! (A hill.)
There He is, once more! (A forest.)
It is He, everywhere –
The One who never shows His face.'

I Squeeze through the Crowd

I try to squeeze through the crowd.
'Stand aside! Make room!
I have wings!'

'Hey, if you've got wings, why in hell don't you fly?'
'My wings are meant only for walking.
They keep my spirits pumped up.
The deep, strong breaths of wind
Protect me from the minor earthquakes
That assault me.

'When I wish to fly,
I do it much more simply.
I reach my hands straight above me
And dive into the blue
That surrounds us.
Into the idea of sky.
Into the idea of flight.'

[28 November 1996]

Don't Hit

Wherever I've travelled
(This is the reason I've been greatly envied,
Sneered at, terrorised, tailed too close for comfort),
As soon as I floated into the sky, gradually soaring above the horizon
So as to contemplate the serene grandeur of the universe,
The peace within its walls,
I'd hear a human, much too familiar,
Don't! Don't hit! (don't hit me).
Screams, groans loud enough to wake the dead,
Sobs of uninterrupted lamentation,
And this *Don't hit!* in every possible language,
Above the seven continents –
This rainbow of black felt,
Wadding hearing with grief.
Finally I asked a watchman,
'What are you doing, gentlemen?
Have you transformed the other world
Into some dark, gloomy dungeon?
Do the heavens have another boundary nearby,
Uncatalogued by theologians?
Why do you torture the poor souls?'

'The toxins are being taken out of them.'

Oh, what an accursed earth!
What smoky air!
I find I'm hearing the word *toxin* more and more often.
I battle against it.
Yet all I can report,
For the sake of everyone, is this *Don't hit!*
Who was it who claimed there are no bridges linking
This world to the world beyond?

[28 November 1996]

Job

'Enough, my pretties!
We've played all day,
I caressed you,
I petted you,
Now it's late!
Let me go to sleep
For a few minutes at least.
I'm dead-tired.
Tomorrow we can start over.'

These girls are the 1500 or 2000 boils
That keep poor Job in their clutches
And play with him as only they know how.
They drag him across the floor, bump his head
Against anything in the way.

He scratches them, scraping
With potsherd and jagged shard of glass.
Many come to mock,
Knowing him at rock bottom.
His flesh smitten with pain, sackcloth itchy upon his skin,
He listens to them and demonstrates
In the subtext the absurdity
Of both his existence and nonexistence –
So, you take the Lord's name in vain,
Faithless man?
'Cursed be the day wherein I was born,
May it perish and be erased from time's span.
But God must not be judged logically:
God must be accepted and experienced.
O Lord, multiply my pains
And take them to the limit!
Later, how else can I be sure to remember
This horrendous affliction,
The year of boils and pustules?!'

[28 November 1996]

'I've become accustomed to sleeping with my eyes open wide'

I've become accustomed to sleeping with my eyes open wide,
For fear I should be taken unawares.
I must be in control of the world
Until the last tick.

Like a lighthouse that will not shut off by day,
I constantly hold the horizon of the sea
In the lantern beam of a desperate stare.

Please, when the time comes,
Close my eyelids gently.
I have seen whatever there was to be seen!
Carefully lower these delicate blinds
Over my weary eyes.

I hope it will be as late as possible
During a night swimming in stars
And acacia trees white with flowers.

[28 November 1996]

I Haven't the Least Idea

I haven't the least idea what to do
With you now,
Thoughts too intimately tied to me.
I meant to burn these lines:
They might masquerade as poetry,
Were they not so desperately true,

And were there not, at the end of the rope
Of every line,
Just myself,
Lost without footing on an infinite field of ice,
Numb with cold and despair,
At the end of my rope.

These toxins would have assassinated me
If I hadn't struggled free of them.
I am surpassingly sorry
To have written you, my lines,
And I still go on hoping
Nobody will ever read you.

[28 November 1996]

Don't Ask Me What Day Today Is

Don't ask me what day today is –
I won't know.
I left home a year ago
And have never gone back.
I believe I stepped out of time, too,
Through a cleft.

I find myself somewhere behind a wall,
Facing another wall
Which could be
Impossibly far from here,
Maybe at the ends of the earth.
You can hear everything through them
But you cannot communicate:
They're not like the walls of a house.

I've never gone back home
Since that May morning
When I allowed myself to be taken away.

Today might be a red-letter day
On all the calendars.
But how would I know? For a year of days
I've been staring at these walls
In search of the crack through which I might return...
And hearing only bells.

[28 November 1996]

'Unable to sleep'

Unable to sleep
I drink my energy from your sleep,
A sleep so telluric, so healthy
It rests me as well. I am the vampire:
You sleep, but I am the dream.
Your power of fancy keeps me whole, lends me strength.
It doesn't matter whether I'm happy or sad –
It's only me, feasting on your energy.
I am the dream.
Good night!

[28 November 1996]

'Whoever sees me hugging the trees'

Whoever sees me hugging the trees
Mustn't be alarmed. We're merely having a tête-à-tête.
I'm asking them to sponsor me
With a little life,
To arrange some of my papers for me –
Trees are very understanding of the leaf problem,
And if I lose mine
All at once,
Never again will they grow back next spring.
Trees have their roots
As deep in the sky as in the earth.
The sun makes its bed in their crown.
I tell them I love the forest madly,
I sang the forest and suffer for it gladly.
I feel like a beast of the wild woods,
Lost in the street, disoriented for a moment.
I urgently need the sympathy
Of these stately trunks,
Which can breathe over me
Their mysterious regenerating haze.

Oh, oak, oh, elm destined to fall,
Oh, beech with your silver bark,
You, fir, cathedral prickly to the touch,
Acacias, hornbeams,
And you once again, oh, secular oak
Struck by lightning several times on your brow,
I'm squeezing you tight in my arms.
Please give me a tender rustle,
You magic flutes, once more fill
My heart with nature's joy.
Certainly, many are the promises that can be made.

[28 November 1996]

The Host of Hell

Devils have entered me:
They abandoned some pigs
At the instant I happened by
And they jostled into my feeble human frame.

There are throngs of them, legions,
Hordes that kick me with unclean hooves
And poke me inside with sharp horns.

The doctors say I have one in every cell.
All my tissues are like thick black felt
Infested with hellish torment.
I squirm and writhe, about to lose my mind.
My friends send me talismans with miniature icons
From Meteora.
My wife reads me prayers and the Book of Job
To buck me up.
She spreads incense in the house and
Says I might as well
Swallow a pinch of myrrh.
In a roundabout way, hinting with parables,
She tries to persuade me
It would be prudent to receive the Eucharist:
Whatever is confessed here
Gets forgiven in the world beyond.
She says it's not improper to receive the Eucharist
If we're good Christians.

My neighbours go to church
And light a candle for me.
From abroad I receive
Telegrams from poets, my friends,
Encouraging me to be strong.
Nevertheless, I remain isolated in my unwillingness,
Goaded from somewhere inside
By flames – I've no idea where they might be contained.

If I lived among savages
And not the indifferent people here,
And if the sorcerers got wind
I was possessed by devils,
They would take me to the banks of a pond,
Tie me to some gnarled roots,
Smoke me with the dry powder of hot peppers,
And beat me, scarify me with their ceremonial knives,

Until all the devils
Flee from me in fury.
As for now, I still have hopes.
I've asked the swineherd
Always to keep in my vicinity
A herd of swine.
I seem to hear the steps of the Good Preacher
Who casts out devils from man with only His Word.

My Poor Skin

It looks as if I've stretched my skin between two sticks
And gone begging with it.
Feast your eyes on it, it's a miracle, oh look:
It fought the sore and got the better of it.

It's a patch of sky
That lived through the hardest of times,
Labouring in the service of
A body that attracted every sort of dust and lint,
All the evil energies.
From now on, it will be spotless, carefree,
It will enjoy
Only soft, sweet breezes
And the nightingale's song therapy.

'I have to sip water after each word I speak'

I have to sip water after each word I speak
Because my mouth gets parched, I don't know why.
In my words exists the full bitterness
Of an autumn day, steady drizzle
Under a dreary, low sky.
They are crushed words,
Woebegone, that make me feel infinite pity.

[30 November 1996]

'With an immense effort of will I get out of bed'

With an immense effort of will I get out of bed.
It's an act of heroism
To shave,
Especially since I find myself shaving a stranger.
Who could it be that stares back at me, spooked,
As if asking me, 'And who are you, Mr Bag-of-Bones?
Does the barber's trade still pay the rent?
What's the going rate these days?'
I have a mind to let my beard grow
And become a hermit,
Withdrawn into the endless cave of night.

[30 November 1996]

Elegy

The light in the eyes has dimmed,
The smile at the corner of the mouth has been extinguished.
But the day isn't dark,
People go by in the streets, laughing merrily.

How good that everything is thus appointed
That I may disappear from the flock while no one's taking heed.
Nothing happens in this world
Except matters of substance, bathed
In indifference.

[30 November 1996]

Then

'Then why such silence,
So impenetrable, so terrifying?'
'Oh, we communicate with those on the other side
All the time. Of course.
But we've nothing more to say.'

[2 December 1996]

Guilt

I feel almost guilty of something,
As if I ought to be bitterly penitent
For having involuntarily seen
Something not supposed to be seen.

From the profound and smiling face
Of the bride (the moon princess),
I had raised the veil for a single instant,
And I was deathly astonished to see,
Instead of a smiling countenance, radiating happiness,
Indeed a bride – but with a contrary sign.

I oughtn't to have come to this ritual wedding.
Let me throw away the white ribbon pinned to my lapel
And hasten to inform the other guests
We've no one to be happy for
In the mists of this cosmic masquerade:
Oh, we should flee from here!

[2 December 1996]

A Glimmer

Every now and then I still summon up
A glimmer of interest in what's around me.

Sometimes I find myself
Watching in wonder
The tops of the birch trees
Clustered in the hospital yard.
I admire their whiteness,
And I like to ask myself
Where their whitewash comes from.

In a marvel of equilibrium
Little birds perch
On twigs so thin
They tremble like strings.

Above, in the blue-violet sky,
Clouds scurry past
Chasing each other aimlessly:
I stare, eyes transfixed
By these strange waves.

In just this way, inside my being,
Clouds of poison circulate,
Scudding toward every azimuth –
For an instant the sky goes blank
As if through magic little windows
I have a brief moment
Of miraculous communication with the world.

[2 December 1996]

The Birches

The birches send me letters:
'Be brave, forget this dirty trick,
Don't go out on a limb, bend with the wind,
Stay planted where you are, keep on working!

'And when you need writing paper,
Avail yourself of our bark,
Supple and white.
It's much better than papyrus.
If you cannot come get it,
Write upon us, long distance, through the window.
We preserve everything in our living library.'

[3 December 1996]

My Glasses

Daringly I lower myself
Into the armchair, and
With a great deal of effort I adjust
The book on my knees.
But then, sick at heart, I notice
My glasses far away,
Across the room on my desk.
How can I make them come to me
On their own?
From four metres,
What magnet can attract them?

Until not long ago
I myself was an extraordinary magnet.
All the things I wished for
Were pleased to come to me –
Or I would go to them.
I seemed even happier
To employ the inverse of my power of attraction
And allow myself to be drawn elsewhere
On wings of air.

Oh, I have covered a goodly portion of this Earth
With these feet;
When I reflect on
The pressopuncture I experienced
On the loftiest of mountains, how I climbed
To the peaks of lunar volcanoes
(Of you, too, I hope to sing one day, Teide),
I begin to feel almost dizzy.

Today the book weighs heavily on my knees,
And my glasses won't fly
To me.

If I doze, coughing will choke me again.

[3 December 1996]

A Thought for the Greek

We would, it's true, be mere appearances
But for pain –
Brute, physical pain
That muffles the deepest
Roars of the soul.
And when it grows unbearable
Or lasts longer than we thought it ever could,
We become inexpressibly concrete
Behind the bars of our existence.

I too passed the mouth of your cave.
The cave suspected
I might be a shadow lit from behind,
And so on and so forth.
We are, in fact, a system of shadows
That modify and magnify along our way.

We step ahead and pass
The mouth of your cave,
Men and women with flaming torches in our hands.

[3 December 1996]

The Dragon

The belt snake
Has captured me somehow,
A vanished serpent
Resurrected from a treatise on zoology
Because this was what the Fate predicted
When her mind drifted elsewhere,
Forgetting that dragons no longer exist.
Now the snake's prey is waiting on line.
Ahead of him, at various stages
Of dissolution by saliva and digestive fluids,
Other valiant men.
All of them screamed, flailed frantically,
Then composed their thoughts while
They advanced as though on a conveyor belt.
The final one, already at its feet,
Still harbours aspirations.
In the meantime the snake is shedding its skin.
With extraordinary effort
It removes its tunic of armour scales.
The skin reeks horribly of garlic.
He watches as it sparkles
With thousands of reflections:
'I've been offered the chance to see a last
Sunset,' he tells himself, 'and it's like a miracle.'

[3 December 1996]

'Oh, how heavy my coat is'

Oh, how heavy my coat is,
As if it were armour for a tournament
In which, proud knight,
I have often taken part.

Oh, how heavy these shoes are,
As if they were dragging along
All the earth I have trod.

Oh, how hard it is to dream.
A blind has been rolled down
And I spend the entire night
Imageless.

Oh, how heavy everything is,
Hard and heavy!

[3 December 1996]

Guilt

I feel guilty
As though
I'd done something wrong.

At the great confession
Awaiting me
I shall speak up as follows:

O Lord,
I lived
Among your creatures.
Was that wrong?

The Wise Man

Afflicted as I was,
I stepped into the Vale of Tears.
'Did you step right foot first, or left?'
'My left.'
'That's bad.'
'And if I'd stepped with my right first,
It would have been just as bad.
It's the same difference.
Better not step
Into the Vale of Tears.'

Now my horse has turned tail
And galloped home on its own.

'So this is it'

So this is it –
The hour.

I don't know what
To do first,
How I'm supposed to behave.

They tell me
I screamed in desperation
For three days at birth.

If it weren't
For these pains, I'd have said
This is a good death.

Spirit

Next to the cross
There also was
A letterbox –
He still received
Correspondence.

He read it, well after midnight,
When He climbed down
To give His bones a shake
And take a deep breath of fresh air.

He read without opening the envelopes:
He continued to refine His spirit
And always kept in touch with the world –
The world it was that recoiled from Him.

'God, it's not good sportsmanship'

God, it's not good sportsmanship
To bring down the horse
The moment
He clears the hurdle.

That extraordinary effort,
The frenzy of the race,
The ears,
The eyes filled with the promised light,

The glistening flanks
Steaming, the knotted tail...
He could see himself crossing
The finish line first,
A length
Ahead of Conrad,
When, all of a sudden, You bring him down
With a flick of Your finger.

The Ram with Coiled Horns

The ram with coiled horns,
Twisted 24 times on each side,
Steps back, aims straight before him
And smashes headfirst into the foot of the bridge.

He fights fiercely with the bridge,
The glorious ram with coiled horns.

Bloodied, he sinks to his knees and proclaims:
'I have smashed into the bounds of knowledge.
I battled proudly, but
I could not force it farther away,
It would not budge...

'Fear of death impelled me.
Bravery made me charge with my horns.
Alas, in vain.

'The foot of this bridge is death...
And my ram's head suffers.

'Oh, sun, our every hope is in you,
You who...'
Great tears drop from his beautiful
Ram's eyes.
His horns glitter powerlessly
Coiled 24 times.

Departure

I turn to face
The wall
And say to my friends
Who grieve:
I'll be back in no time.

Separation from Myself

Dialogue

'Ah, how I'd have liked it if…'

The Unforeseen

'I'm unusually healthy, I can
Live, God
Help me, till I'm 90.'
'Haven't you heard about the unforeseen?
Read the parable of the rich man
Whose ground brought forth plentifully.'

Experiment

They submerged me
In a liquid
And forgot
To pull me out.

It's true that I didn't
Displace a greater and greater volume,
My volume being for the present
Drastically diminished.

They tell me
I should paddle with my hands
And kick hard.
Science doesn't have
Sufficient funds
During this period of austerity.

[5 December 1996]

A Turn for the Better

It's good, O Lord,
That You thought of me
And didn't choose somebody else
For Your delicate, frightful
Experiment.

I knew I could stand up to the worst
And I boasted
That deep inside I had
Inexhaustible energy.

I fell into the sin of pride.
Forgive me,
It's human –
Avert Your glance likewise
From my other sins.

I believed that the life granted me
Really was mine,
That I really was myself,
Perhaps sometimes forgetting You.

Now, beginning to take a turn for the better,
Or so those who see me say,
I must be treading on Your coattails of rainbow.
To the totality of my fright,
I've come to add the precious stone of humility,
And I bring to the Creator of light
My praise of magnificence and glory.

[5 December 1996]

Prayer of the Heart

Lord,
Help me as long as
I still live.

Set my heart in order,
Put me at peace with the world
And the miracle of life.

Remove from my mind
The fixed idea
Which has imprisoned me.

Make of my subconscious
A torrent of hope.

[5 December 1996]

'In my prayers I've reached the point'

In my prayers I've reached the point
That I no longer ask God
For a few years, or for one year,
But I ask merely for one day,
For one night:

'Lord, help me pass through
This new night.
Lord, make this next day
More bearable.'

[5 December 1996]

'I've turned my subconscious toward the plus'

I've turned my subconscious toward the plus.
It had faced the minus
Enclosed in a circle
Exactly at the core of the Earth.
Daily it irradiated me
With pulses of grief.
'Stop this nonsense at once,' I told it.
'I'm a solar man,
I need emanations from above.
I felt good in the air,
In the joy
Of a fulfilling life.'

'There's an attraction for Thanatos, too,'
A fascination replies to me.
'Always farther and farther thresholds to cross.
Leave things for later.
Come out into the light,
We'll do fine, old fellow!'

[7 December 1996]

News

With a touch of irony,
Newspapers inform their readers
About my painful state.
Yes, I'm taking morphine,
Yes, I'm spending
My last days in the countryside.
I haven't the time to give explanations
Or issue denials.
I haven't the strength.
'The reports of my death
Are greatly exaggerated,'
Mark Twain said,
Emerging from an illness himself.
Anyhow, why
Be ashamed
Of suffering?
Even the savage beasts
Won't attack each other
Drinking at the water-hole.

[7 December 1996]

The Switch

The tram tracks pass by the hospital,
And directly in front of my room
The switch is thrown.
I've become used to this railroad noise.
But sometimes at night
It startles me.
Sometimes at night, when
With difficulty I've barely dozed off,
It sounds like bombardment.
It seems to me that a man gets down from every train
And runs here
To bring me news.
He knocks at my door:
'Who is it?' I ask, full of hope,
'Come in!'
'It's me, the switch.
I must tell you that the No. 14 tram, too, has passed on.'

[7 December 1996]

'I am reminded of all our dogs'

I am reminded of
All our dogs
When it came time to die
Of old age.
They would lie hidden under the shed,
Under the corn crib.
You'd take them food, water.
Slowly, they would open their eyelids,
They would look, they would raise their eyes
Toward you,
Then they would close them once again.
And they couldn't even wag
Their tail once,
To thank you.

Terrible is the passage
Into the fold
Both for man and for animal.

[7 December 1996]

Addenda

Bird Pilot

Am I the pilot
For the birds?
Why do they follow me like this?

On Every Facet

My quartz crystal
Glimmers with only hope.

*   *   *

Full of curiosity, I keep an eye on myself,
With emotion and a certain fear.

*   *   *

They come to say goodbye.

*   *   *

At night, in order to sleep,
I should take the moon
As a pill.
So great is
My unrest.

NOTE ON THE TRANSLATORS

Adam J. Sorkin's previous two Bloodaxe translations, *The Triumph of the Water Witch*, prose poems by Ioana Ieronim (2000, translated jointly with Ieronim) and *The Sky Behind the Forest: Selected Poems* by Liliana Ursu (1997, translated with Ursu and Tess Gallagher), were both shortlisted for the Weidenfeld Prize. Other volumes of his poetry translations from the Romanian include a book of Ieronim's short poems, *41* (2003, translated with Ieronim), *Speaking the Silence: Prose Poets of Contemporary Romania* (2001) and two 1999 collections, *Sea-Level Zero*, poems by Daniela Crăsnaru largely translated with the poet, and *Bebop Baby*, poems by Mircea Cărtărescu. He has won the *International Quarterly* Crossing Boundaries Translation Award, the Kenneth Rexroth Memorial Translation Prize, and honours in Romania in Cluj, Iași, and Satu Mare, and his work has been awarded Fulbright, IREX, Academy of American Poets, Witter Bynner Foundation for Poetry, and Rockefeller Foundation grants. Sorkin is Distinguished Professor of English at Penn State University.

Lidia Vianu, a Romanian poet, novelist, critic, and translator, has published four books of literary criticism, the most recent, *British Desperadoes at the Turn of the Millennium* (1999), a book of interviews, *Censorship in Romania* (1997), one novel, *Prisoner in the Mirror* (1993), and three poetry collections, *1, 2, 3* (1997), *Moderato 7* (1998) and *Very* (2001), as well as five translated volumes (into both Romanian and English) and five anthologies of British and American literature and criticism. She has been twice been Fulbright lecturer in Comparative Literature, at the State University of New York, Binghamton, NY, and the University of California, Berkeley, and she has been awarded a grant from the Soros Foundation. Her translations with Adam J. Sorkin have been widely published. Vianu is Professor of English at the University of Bucharest.